Birds & flowers
ALBUM

Bea Oglesby

American Quilter's Society
P. O. Box 3290 • Paducah, KY 42002-3290
www.AQSquilt.com

Located in Paducah, Kentucky, the American Quilter's Society (AQS) is dedicated to promoting the accomplishments of today's quilters. Through its publications and events, AQS strives to honor today's quiltmakers and their work and to inspire future creativity and innovation in quiltmaking.

EDITOR: BARBARA SMITH
GRAPHIC DESIGN: ELAINE WILSON
COVER DESIGN: MICHAEL BUCKINGHAM
PHOTOGRAPHY: CHARLES R. LYNCH

Library of Congress Cataloging-in-Publication Data
Oglesby, Bea, 1924–
    Birds & flowers album / by Bea Oglesby.
        p. cm.
        ISBN 1-57432-819-0
    1. Appliqué--Patterns.   2. Embroidery--Patterns.   3.
Quilting--Patterns.   I. Title: Birds and flowers album.   II. Title.
    TT779.O33   2003
    746.46'041--dc21

                        2003002586

Additional copies of this book may be ordered from the American Quilter's Society, PO Box 3290, Paducah, KY 42002-3290; 800-626-5420 (orders only please); or online at www.AQSquilt.com. For all other inquiries, call 270-898-7903.

OPPOSITE PAGE: VIEW FROM MY KITCHEN WINDOW (39½" x 31½").
Row 1: Chimney Swift, p. 34; Purple Martin, p. 62.
Row 2: Barn Swallow, p. 22; Scissor-Tailed Flycatcher, p. 72.

Dedication

To my three daughters, Corinne, Janet, and Elise,
who each in their own way gave me advice and help in
containing my never ending flow of ideas, and to my
husband, Red, my ever patient helpmate, I love you all.

Acknowledgments

Thanks to...

the Johnson County, Kansas, librarians for their patience and assistance with my research on the birds for this book;

all my quilting students, who taught me as much as I was teaching them;

the local quilt shops for their advice in helping me to find just the perfect fabric for a certain bird's wing or tail;

the staff of the American Quilter's Society for giving me the opportunity to share my love of nature and quilting.

BIRDERS' DELIGHT (32" x 32").
Row 1: Black Phoebe, p. 26; Yellow Warbler, p. 84.
Row 2: Purple Finch, p. 60; Mourning Dove, p. 54.

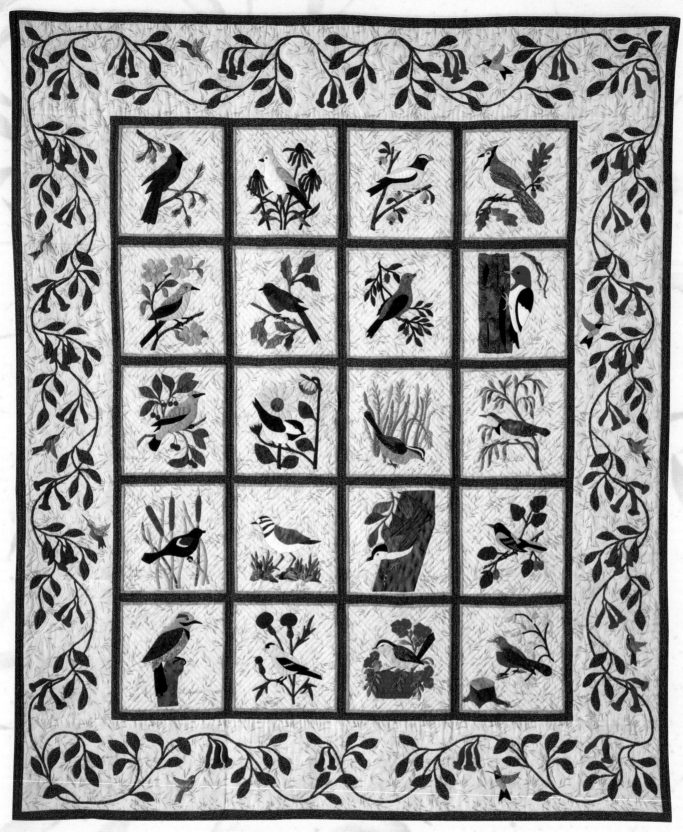

Backyard Birds and Flowers (72" x 86").

Row 1: Northern Cardinal, p. 56; Tufted Titmouse, p. 76; Evening Grosbeak, p. 44; Blue Jay, p. 28.

Row 2: Northern Mockingbird, p. 58; Eastern Bluebird, p. 40; Scarlet Tanager, p. 70; Red-Headed Woodpecker, p. 64.

Row 3: Cedar Waxwing, p. 32; Black-Capped Chickadee, p. 24; Chipping Sparrow, p. 36; Eastern Meadowlark, p. 42.

Row 4: Red-Winged Blackbird, p. 66; Killdeer, p. 52; White-Breasted Nuthatch, p. 78; Baltimore Oriole, p. 20.

Row 5: Yellow-Shafted Flicker, p. 82; American Goldfinch, p. 16; Carolina Wren, p. 30; American Robin, p. 18.

Contents

Preface

I cannot imagine a backyard without trees, shrubs, and flowers, nor a backyard without birds in those trees, shrubs, and flowers. I am not a birder, but I do watch the birds from my windows. My family and I have lived in many areas of this country, from south Florida to Maryland, to upstate New York, Illinois, California and now Kansas. Though not an expert gardener, I always try to have flowers and plants in my yard that are native to the area, and with these plants, the birds have come.

In south Florida, our birds were different from the birds in upstate New York. While living in Florida, I never saw a Baltimore oriole, but they were familiar in New York. In Florida I was more familiar with the scrub jay, which has no crest, than with the crested blue jay. In California, the hummingbirds were numerous, but here in Kansas, I must be on the alert to see one. While living in a wooded area in Illinois, I became familiar with many different woodpeckers from the small downy to the large flicker, and it was in Illinois that I saw my first bluebird. It made my day.

You too can be successful in attracting a variety of birds to your yard. Besides plants and flowers, birds need a little encouragement. Food and water are the main attractions for them, and I am amazed at the number of the different grains and seeds and the different feeders that are available for wild birds. One year for Father's Day, my husband received a cookbook from our daughter called *My Recipes Are for the Birds*. I'll admit that it hasn't been used too much, however the names of some of the recipes are fascinating, such as Cardinal Casserole, Dove Delight, and Mockingbird Muffins. We do not buy the common wild bird seed mix from the grocery store. We buy seeds, such as sunflower, millet, and thistle, and of course we get suet to attract a variety of guests. My husband keeps the birdbath filled and even bought a heater for it to keep the water from freezing in the winter.

Appliqué is my favorite form of quilting, and what better way to enjoy nature and quilting than to design and make a bird quilt. Most of the birds in my quilts will be familiar to you, and you have probably seen many of them in your own backyard. I have enjoyed studying birds and drawing them and have combined some of them with familiar plants and flowers into appliqué block patterns. I hope you will enjoy them.

Introduction

These bird patterns can be used as a single design or combined to make a wallhanging or a full-sized quilt. All of the designs can fit on a background as small as 9" by 12" except for the scissor-tailed flycatcher, because of its tail. They can be appliquéd on larger backgrounds to increase the size of a quilt or wallhanging. The birds on the large quilt and on the four-block wallhanging were appliquéd on 12" squares. The two individual hummingbird wallhangings were each appliquéd on a 9" by 12" background. On two wallhangings, the birds were perched on branches surrounded by leaves, with the exception of the chimney swift, which is flying in the air. The birds in these two wallhangings can be done as a single block on a branch or made into a wallhanging, as I did. Many of these birds can be interchanged to make a quilt with your favorite birds that will be uniquely yours.

All of the blocks were hand appliquéd by using the freezer paper method. If you are familiar with another appliqué method, feel free to use whatever you prefer. If you are new to appliqué, I would advise taking a basic class. The patterns are not difficult, but some experience is necessary. The pieces in the bird patterns range from four pieces in the red-winged blackbird to thirteen pieces in the killdeer. The flowers, plants, and branches make up the rest of the pattern. I used both embroidery and appliqué for the birds' beaks, eyes, and claws. It depended on the size of the piece. Some of the claws clutching the branches were just too small to appliqué, so embroidery was used. In my tips given for each bird, I described what I did. If the bird had many small pieces next to each other, such as the rings on the neck of the killdeer and the stripes on the head of the downy woodpecker, I appliquéd those pieces together as a unit then appliquéd the unit to the background.

The amount of material needed for your project will depend on what you plan to make. A piece of fabric as small as 10" by 14" is all that is needed for one block. However if a large quilt is wanted, you will have to decide on the size of the background block and multiply it by the number of blocks needed. Be generous in your estimate, because it is better to be safe than sorry. Leftover fabric can always be used in another project.

For each of these thirty-five birds, a color photograph and a full-sized pattern is included. The fabrics chosen were for the male birds because, for the most part, they are the most colorful. Some females have the same coloring but most do not. I also took some liberties with my color choices if I needed a contrast between the bird and the background. Feel free to do the same.

FEATHERED FRIENDS (31" x 31").
Clockwise from top-left: Tree Swallow, p. 74; Rose-Breasted Grosbeak, p. 68;
Downy Woodpecker, p. 38; Wood Thrush, p. 80; Indigo Bunting, p. 50.

General Instructions

Tools and Supplies

One of the advantages of appliqué is that minimal equipment is needed to complete a project. Other than background and appliqué fabrics, you will need only basic sewing supplies. For this reason, I always suggest that you buy the best quality available. These supplies, once purchased, will last a good many years, and some will last a lifetime if properly cared for. As you build up your tool supply, remember that they are a good investment, and they will not only make your work easier but will also improve it.

NEEDLES

For appliqué, I suggest sharps or straw needles, which come in various sizes. The smaller the needle the better, because a small needle is easier to push through fabric. Needles are numbered according to size. The higher the number, the smaller the needle. A size 12 needle is smaller than a size 9 needle. Sharps are a little longer than betweens, which are usually used for quilting. Some people prefer the straw needles, sometimes called milliner's needles. They are longer than the sharps. I cannot adjust to their length and find that they bend easily. I use a sharp, size 11. It has a narrow shank and does not leave holes in the fabric. Although the needle eye is small, the thread I use is so fine that threading the needle is not a problem.

THREAD

There are many different threads on the market, and one spool of all-purpose thread will not suffice. Today there are not only many different brands of thread, but there are different types within the brands. You will need different threads for machine appliqué and hand appliqué, as well as different threads for machine sewing and for quilting. If you are not familiar with the different threads, I recommend that you spend some time reading spool labels and talking to the experts in the shops. For hand appliqué, I always use 100 percent cotton thread and try to match it in color to the appliqué piece as closely as possible. I do not recommend cotton-wrapped polyester thread because it frays easily, and it is more difficult to thread through a needle. Remember, when buying thread, that the higher the thread number, the finer the thread. For instance, a #30 thread is much heavier and thicker than a # 60 thread.

THIMBLES

A thimble is a necessary tool. Without one, it is almost impossible to get the desired stitch quality in your work. There are many thimble types available, including metal, plastic, and leather. There are even pads to position on your finger in place of a thimble. If you have a favorite, there is no need to change. When shopping for a thimble, be sure it is strong and has deep enough dimples to keep the blunt end of the needle from slipping as you take your stitches. Also, be sure to try the thimble on for size before you buy it, because nothing is more frustrating than one that is too tight or one that falls off with every movement. I use a standard metal thimble with a small rim around the top.

PINS

One pin size does not fit all needs. I use three different types for my work. I have a box of large pins with yellow plastic heads, called quilt pins. These are used to hold batting and backing together and to hold quilt blocks and tops on my design wall. They are not for use in appliqué or hand sewing because they are entirely too large. For appliqué, I mainly use fine silk pins with glass heads. They are smooth and sharp, and they do not leave holes in the fabric. They have glass heads, which make them easy to pick up from your pincushion or from your fabric. I also use the small ¾" appliqué pins with glass heads. These are handy to use for small appliqué pieces. The ones without the glass heads are difficult to handle and inconvenient to use.

SCISSORS

Scissors are a long-term investment, but with care, they will last a lifetime. To keep a sharp edge on your scissors, use them only on cloth and never on paper. I have two 5" pairs. I like this size for cutting fabric because, while it is a little larger than embroidery scissors, it is still small enough to go around curves. It's also a good size for cutting small pieces, and the points are sharp enough for snipping curves and notches. My other pair of 5" scissors is used for paper and plastic. They have a bright colored handle, so that I am able to tell the two apart. I also use appliqué scissors for trimming away the excess fabric from behind the appliqué pieces. These scissors, sometimes called "pelican bill," have one narrow blade and one wide semicircular blade. These are not a necessity; however, if you do much appliqué, they are handy and the shape of the blade enables you to cut away the back fabric without poking through and cutting the front.

MARKERS

There is no one perfect marking pen or pencil, and there are many different types available. What works on one fabric may not work on another. To test a marker, try it on your fabric and see if it will brush off or wash out. If it doesn't, try another. For light backgrounds, I like to use a .5 mm super-thin-lead quilter's pencil. It is always sharp and it doesn't smear, but it is a little difficult to wash out. However, the line is so light and thin that it is easy to cover with your appliqué. For dark fabrics, I like a white chalk pencil. The lines will brush or erase off. These pencils can be sharpened like any pencil. There are other chalk pencils of various colors that you may need for floral or different fabrics. Marking pencils are not expensive, so you can have an assortment. The main thing to remember is to test each marker before using it on your project. Do not iron any of your pieces until the markings have been removed, because heat will set the markings.

BACKGROUND FABRIC

I use 100 percent cotton of good quality and an even weave for all my background fabrics. The background for the bird quilt or any of the wallhangings can be either light or dark. It can be plain or have an overall discreet or muted pattern, but care must be taken so that the print will not dominate the appliqué pattern nor distract from it. I prefer an overall pattern to plain fabric for my backgrounds, because it gives the quilt dimension. I used a muted leaf pattern for the large quilt. It has an off-white background with pale, grayish green leaves. On the wallhangings, I used either mottled fabrics or muted prints. Choose a background that you are comfortable with both in color and design.

APPLIQUÉ FABRIC

Again, I use 100 percent cotton for my appliqué. Cotton is the easiest fabric to use because it keeps a crease, it is not slippery to work with, and it does not ravel. Rayon, silk, and polyester are lovely fabrics; however, they are hard to handle and difficult to needle-turn. For the bird appliqué, I found that geometric prints, both large and small, worked well. Also, I used many mottled, hand-dyed, and batik fabrics for the birds' bodies. For the flowers and leaves, I used prints and floral fabrics, both large and small. I usually do not use solid colors because I believe they make the appliqué appear flat. With the vast array of fabrics on the market today, many different looks can be achieved.

Appliqué Tips

PREPARING THE BACKGROUND

Thoroughly wash and rinse all fabrics to be used. Remove the fabric from the dryer while still damp and iron it dry. Add 2" to the desired size of your finished block. If you want your finished block to be 12" x 12", cut your background squares 14" x 14". If you want your wallhanging to be 25" square, cut your background 27" square. After the appliqué is finished, the block or wallhanging will be trimmed to size.

Spray the background with starch and iron it dry before you mark the appliqué pattern on it. The starch gives body to the fabric and keeps the fabric from wrinkling as you mark. I also find that the markings wash out more easily because they stay on the surface and do not become embedded in the warp and weft of the fabric.

Place the pattern on a flat surface and use masking tape on the corners to keep it in place. Center your background fabric over the pattern and use tape on the corners to keep it from slipping. If your background is dark, a light box or window may be necessary to see the pattern through the fabric. Again, use masking tape on the corners to keep the fabric from slipping. Draw the complete pattern, with your choice of marking pencil, on the background block.

PREPARING THE APPLIQUÉS

To create appliqué templates, use a pencil to trace the individual pieces on the dull side of a sheet of freezer paper. Mark each template with its number, then cut the pieces exactly on the line. Do not add turn-under allowances to the templates. Position freezer paper templates on the right side of the desired fabrics and press them in place with a dry iron. Then cut the fabric pieces, adding a ¼" turn-under allowance by eye as you cut.

For special fabric effects, you can create window templates instead of using freezer paper. I make them from 4" x 5" notepad sheets. Use the following steps to make a window template:

⭢ To make a window template for a bird's wing, tail, or body piece, trace the pattern in the center of a note-pad sheet.

⭢ Cut the piece out and discard it, creating a window.

⭢ Move the window around on your fabric until you find the desired effect.

⭢ Place the freezer paper pattern in this window, remove the window and iron the freezer paper pattern onto the right side of the fabric.

⭢ Using a marker that will wash out or brush off, trace around the pattern piece on the fabric.

⭢ Cut out the piece with a ¼" turn-under allowance.

On outside curves, you may have to trim a little closer so that the allowance will not pucker or pleat. On inside curves, clip every ¼" along the entire curve so that the allowance will lie flat. These pieces are now ready to appliqué onto the background in numerical order.

SEW THE APPLIQUÉ

Starting with piece #1, with the freezer paper pattern still on the piece, turn the allowance to the back and, using your thumb and forefinger, crease the fabric on the sewing line around the entire piece. Now remove the freezer paper. By using cotton fabric, the crease will remain and the allowance will easily needle turn with the appliqué stitch. I use one pin to hold the piece in place unless it is a very large piece or a long tree branch. If necessary, I clip and trim turn-under allowances close to the fold line as I sew. With tiny and close appliqué stitches, I am able to sew sharp points and gentle smooth curves.

To get the coloring correct in some of the birds, I appliquéd small pieces together as a unit, then appliquéd the unit to the background. To make units, mark carefully around the pattern pieces on the fabric. Stitch these pieces together exactly on the sewing line. Do not stitch the turn-under allowances, just the sewing lines. This will leave the allowances free so they can be turned under smoothly.

In some patterns you will have many pieces to sew together, such as the neck of the killdeer, and in some cases, you will have only two pieces, such as the throat of the blue jay. Other birds for which I used this technique include the sparrow, flicker, barn swallow, and downy woodpecker.

When the appliqué is finished, you can use the following method to cut away the background fabric from under large pieces: From the back of the fabric, separate the two layers and, leaving a ¼" seam allowance, trim out the background fabric. Be careful that you do not cut into the appliqué. This trimming will keep the piece from becoming too heavy or bulky and will make the piece easier to quilt.

Finishing

After the block or wallhanging has been appliquéd, wash out any markings that show before you press the piece. Usually, the heat of the iron will set the markings. On a soft padded surface, press the entire block from the back. This padded surface will keep the embroidery from becoming flat. Trim the finished block or wallhanging to the desired size.

LEFT: ALLEN'S HUMMINGBIRD (12" x 14½"), p. 46.

OPPOSITE PAGE: RUBY-THROATED HUMMINGBIRD (12" x 14½"), p. 48.

Patterns

American Goldfinch

American goldfinches are also known as wild canaries. I was not familiar with these small birds until my husband placed a Niger seed tube feeder right outside my kitchen window. While I was standing at the kitchen sink one day, in front of my face, six or more bright yellow little birds were happily pecking at the seed. I did not intimidate them at all, and I had a front-row seat to watch their antics.

These five-inch long birds flock together in a care-free manner. In the northern states, they usually arrive in the early spring, but here in Kansas, I have seen them all year long. They do not breed until late summer, and this is probably because they wait until the thistles reach full bloom. The birds eat a few insects, but their diet consists primarily of seeds from garden plants, and their favorites are dandelion and thistle seeds.

They weave their nests of sturdy plant fibers and line them with thistle down for a soft, thick mattress. They have only one brood a year, and the female lays four to six eggs. While she incubates the eggs, the male is in constant attendance and brings her food of seeds and insects. He helps to feed the young once they have hatched.

17 appliqué pieces

Color notes

I used one green fabric for the thistle stalks and leaves. The thistle flowers were done in a rich mottled purple fabric, while the bird was appliquéd in a bright gold with a deeper gold for the beak. Black was used for the head, wing, and tail.

Embroidered details

Eye: satin-stitch with two strands of black floss

Legs and claws: stem-stitch with two strands of black floss

Wing markings: stem-stitch with two strands of white floss

American Goldfinch
BACKYARD BIRDS AND FLOWERS, photo p. 6
Add turn-under allowances.

American Robin

The American robin is one of our most familiar birds. We sing songs about robins, read stories to our children about robins, and talk of their red breasts. We watch for the first robin of spring. We know, when we see one, that winter will soon be over. Now that may be true in upstate New York, but here in the Midwest, we have robins year-round. The robin is a medium-sized bird of eight to nine inches in length. It has a dark brown or dark gray body with a speckled white throat, and a rust or brick colored breast, not red. Both sexes look similar, except the male has a darker head than the female.

They nest early in the spring. The female builds a nest of grass, weeds, and yarn or string and lines it with grass and mud. The blue eggs are incubated by the female, but after the eggs hatch, both parents feed worms and insects to the young. The birds' diet is well-known for the earthworms and insects they collect; however, about 60 percent of their diet is vegetable matter, including fruits and berries. A filled birdbath and a feeder with bits of fruit and slices of apple are a robin's dream.

53 appliqué pieces

Color notes

Appliqué the stems first with one shade of brown. Use three shades of yellow for the blossoms to distinguish the petals from each other. The bird has two shades of dark brown. The beak is tan, the throat is speckled, and the breast is rust or brick colored.

Construction tip

The tree stump is optional.

Embroidered details

Eye: satin-stitch with two strands of black floss surrounded by white

Legs and claws: stem-stitch with two strands of brown floss

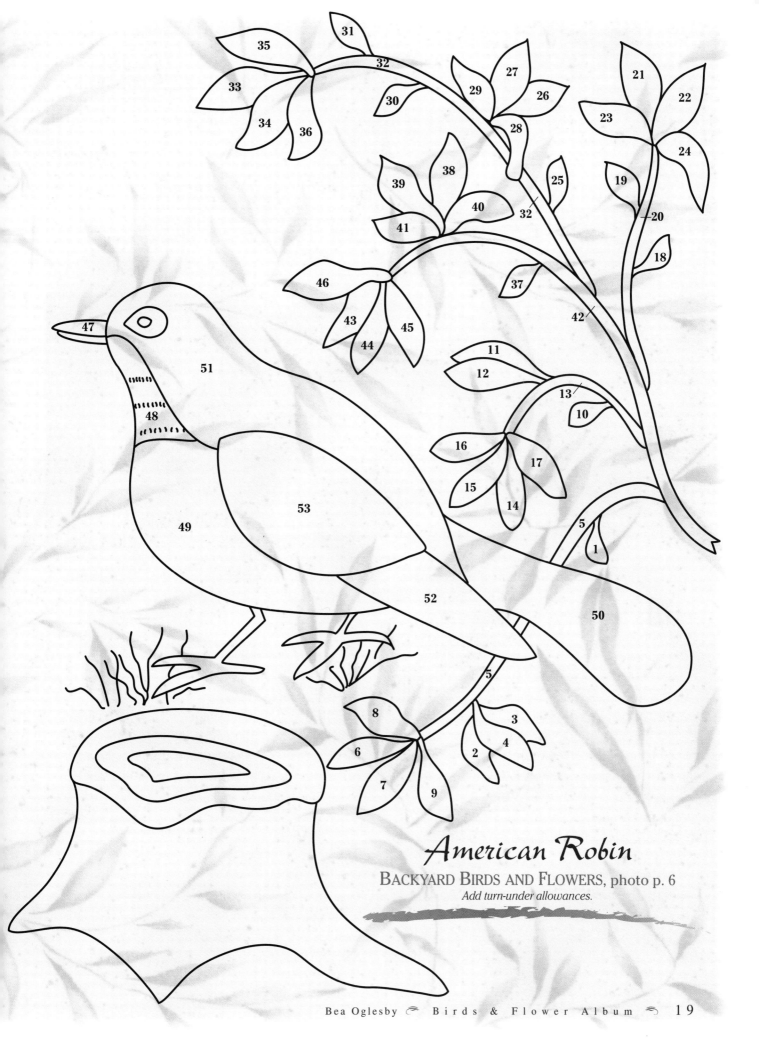

American Robin

BACKYARD BIRDS AND FLOWERS, photo p. 6
Add turn-under allowances.

Baltimore Oriole

The Baltimore oriole is a beautiful bird with spectacular coloring. The male has a brilliant orange and black body. The female is more subdued with olive green on her back and yellow orange on her breast. I have yet to see an oriole in the Midwest, but I did see them when we lived in Maryland and in upstate New York.

The male begins courtship by showing off his colors, and shortly after courtship, the female begins to build her nest. The nest is one of the most beautiful of all bird nests. It is a skillfully woven three- to eight-inch long pouch of plant fibers, string, yarn, cloth, and whatever else the bird can find. The nest is suspended near the end of a drooping branch where it sways in the breeze like a cradle.

The female lays four to six eggs, and she incubates them by herself while the male stands guard. Both parents take part in feeding the young. Insects, including caterpillars, weevils, beetles, and aphids, make up their main diet, but they do like sweets. Wild fruits, such as mulberries, are one of their favorites, and on occasion, they have been known to drink nectar from tubular flowers and to visit nectar feeders.

21 appliqué pieces

Color notes

The branches of the mulberry bush are appliquéd in one shade of brown. One shade of a mottled green was used for the leaves and one shade of purple for the mulberries. The oriole was done in a golden orange and black with a dark gray for the beak.

Embroidered details

Wing markings: stem-stitch with two strands of white floss

Legs and claws: stem-stitch with two strands of black floss

Eye: satin-stitch with two strands of black floss, surrounded by ring of gray floss

Baltimore Oriole

BACKYARD BIRDS AND FLOWERS, photo p. 6
Add turn-under allowances.

Barn Swallow

The barn swallow is about the best known of all the swallows. Smaller than most other swallows, they make up for their size with a streamlined body built for speed and maneuverability to catch insects. They eat and drink on the wing.

The bird's name comes from its habit of nesting in barns and stables. These buildings are decreasing in number, but the birds have adapted by building their nests under bridges, on cliffs, or in the rafters and trusses of many buildings. The nests, which both parents build, are made of mud and straw. Pairs of swallows return each year to the same nesting site and will sometimes repair an old nest rather than build from scratch. Both parents incubate the four to six eggs and share in the feeding of the babies.

15 appliqué pieces

Color notes

The bird's coloring is unusual with its navy blue back, rust-colored throat, and light breast. Pieces #9 and #11 in the tail are white.

Construction tip

The easiest way to make the bird is to appliqué pieces #4, #5, and #6 together as a unit, then appliqué the unit to the background.

Embroidered details

Eye: satin-stitch with two strands of black floss, surrounded by a ring of gray
Claws: stem-stitch with two strands of black floss

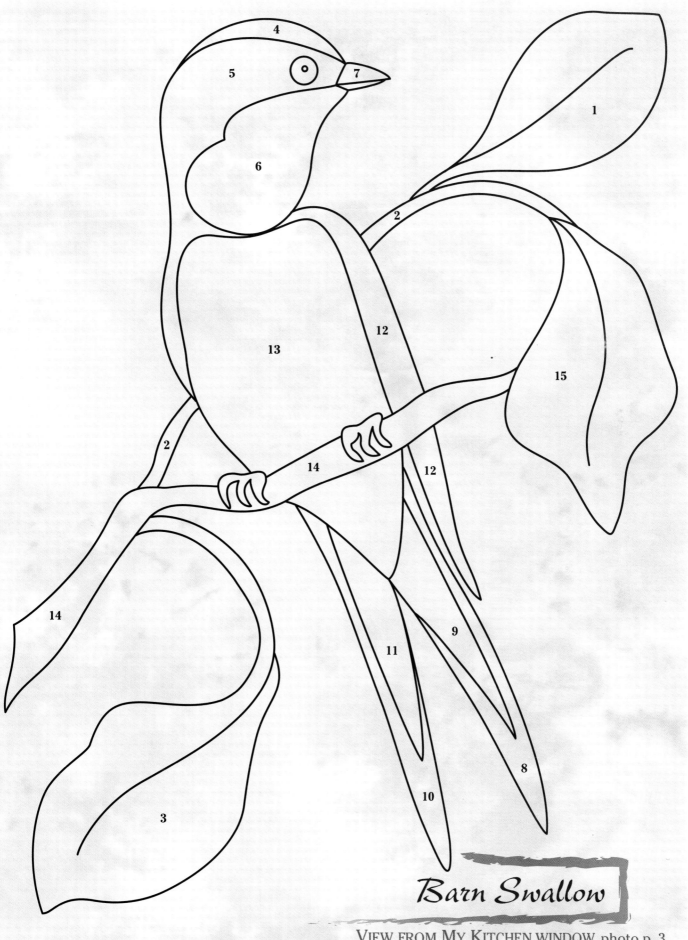

Barn Swallow

Black-Capped Chickadee

This little bird is one of my favorites because it is filled with boundless energy, and it is friendly, cheerful, and good-natured. A patient little bird, it will wait its turn at the feeder until all is clear. The little acrobat seems about as comfortable upside-down on a tree as right side up.

Chickadees usually mate for life and have one or two broods a year. Both the male and female work at chipping out a cavity for their nest, and the female lines the nest with moss, feathers, and animal fur before laying five to eight eggs. While she incubates the eggs, the male brings her meals of insects. Although most of their diet consists of insects, in the summer they will eat seeds and wild fruit, and they will visit your feeder for sunflower seeds and suet in the winter.

49 appliqué pieces

Color notes

I used two shades of gold for the sunflower, and two shades of green, one for the stalks and one for the leaves. A mottled fabric of white and pale yellow was used for the cheeks and breast. Black fabric for the cap and bib and dark gray for wing and tail complete the bird.

Construction tips

Although there are quite a few pieces in this pattern, most of them are sunflower petals, which are not difficult. There are only six pieces in the chickadee.

Embroidered details

Eye: satin-stitch with two strands of black floss, surrounded by a ring of gray
Legs and claws: stem-stitch with two strands of black floss

Black-Capped Chickadee

BACKYARD BIRDS AND FLOWERS, photo p. 6

Add turn-under allowances.

Black Phoebe

38 appliqué pieces

Color notes

One brown fabric was used for the tree branches, and one green fabric was used for the leaves. I used a mottled black for the head, wing, tail, and beak. For the breast, the white fabric was lined so there would be no shadowing from the background fabric.

Constructions tip

To line the breast fabric, cut piece #33 from white lightweight muslin, a bit smaller than the pattern. Baste the muslin on the background about one-fourth inch from the raw edge and appliqué the breast fabric over it.

Embroidered details

Eye: satin-stitch with two strands of black floss, surrounded by a ring of gray

Legs and claws: stem-stitch with two strands of black floss

P hoebes are small-sized flycatchers, about the size of a sparrow. The Eastern phoebe that ranges from the East Coast to the foot of the Rockies is a gray bird with a white or very light gray breast. You will find the black phoebe west of the Rockies to California and south to western Texas. The coloring of the bird is dramatic with its slate black head and body and white breast.

The black phoebe is a common garden flycatcher, which keeps mainly to himself except when mating. For nesting, the pair seek a shelter on rocks or under bridges, wherever they have a supply of mud to build a nest. They line this mud nest with grass, fibers, and feathers. Three to six eggs are laid, and the young are ready to leave the nest in about fifteen days. The male teaches the young to catch their food, while the female prepares for another brood. She can lay up to three broods a year. The phoebe's diet consists mostly of insects, and their favorite food is the common housefly. Your feeders will not attract the birds to your yard, however they do enjoy flowering plants and a water source.

Black Phoebe

BIRDERS' DELIGHT, photo p. 5
Add turn-under allowances.

Blue Jay

T he blue jay is one of the most easily recognized and best known of our backyard birds. It is also one of the easiest to attract to our yards because they will come to any type of feeder and will use our bird baths daily. They have been described as noisy, cunning, and inquisitive. Their behavior also gives the impression that they are more intelligent than most birds. For certain, they are among the boldest and will chase away other birds and plunder their nests. Jays have also been known to chase cats.

The blue jay is a beautiful and showy bird. There is little distinction between the sexes. A mated pair will work together to build their nest of twigs, bark, grass, and paper. The nest is built in the crotch of any handy hardwood or evergreen tree. Both parents are responsible for feeding the young and defending their nest. Jays will take every kind of food offered, including cracked corn, peanut butter, bread, suet, and seeds. In areas where there are oak trees, they will store acorns for winter use.

22 appliqué pieces

Color notes

I used a medium blue for the back. For the wings and tail, I used a deeper blue with a geometric black and white pattern.

Construction tips

The throat (piece #21) and the breast (piece #15) will need to be lined if the background shows through the white fabric. The lining also gives the white fabric a sharp, crisp look. To line these areas, cut the pieces from white lightweight muslin, a bit smaller than the patterns. Baste these muslin pieces on the background about one-fourth inch from their raw edges. Then appliqué the throat and breast pieces on top of the muslin.

I sometimes find it easier to appliqué small pieces together off the background, then treat these combined pieces as one. In this block, I appliquéd the throat (#21) and the necklace (#20) in this way.

Embroidered details

Eye: stem-stitch with two strands of jet black floss

Blue Jay

BACKYARD BIRDS AND FLOWERS, photo p. 6

Add turn-under allowances.

Carolina Wren

These perky little brown birds, with their jaunty tails, are only about four and a half inches long. Although they look rather plain, they are fun to watch because of their vivacious behavior and enthusiastic singing. My first encounter with a wren was on my porch. The bird built its nest in my hanging pot of impatiens, and the female laid her five eggs and nested in with the flowers. We were entertained each day as the eggs hatched, and we watched the male and the female feed the babies and keep house. When the young were ready to leave the nest, the adult went to the porch rail and called for them. One by one the babies left. Wrens are uninhibited around humans, and as a result are easy and fun to watch. Their preferred food is insects, including grasshoppers, beetles, and caterpillars, but they also enjoy soft fruit and berries in the summer.

41 appliqué pieces

Color notes

The leaves and stems can be one green fabric as the leaves do not overlap. A hand-dyed or marbled fabric is desirable for the flowers. Medium brown was used for the bird's wing, tail, and top of head, tan for the body, and a lighter shade for the eye stripe.

Construction tips

Appliqué pieces #1 through #6 first, the pot (piece #7), then finish the other leaves. The flowers are appliquéd in a single piece, with embroidery floss used to distinguish the four petals. Appliqué the bird pieces # 37, # 38 and # 39 together off of the background. Sew this partial bird in place on the background fabric as one piece. Add # 40, the tail, and then # 41, the wing.

Embroidered details

Eye: satin-stitch with two strands of dark brown floss, with a tan French knot in the center
Beak: satin-stitch with two strands, the upper part with dark brown floss and the lower part with tan
Legs: stem-stitch with two strands of dark brown floss
Flowers: a single French knot in each center

Carolina Wren

Add turn-under allowances.

Cedar Waxwing

Although the cedar waxwing is a small bird, only about seven inches long, I consider it a most regal-looking bird. This may be because of the crest on his head, but also because of his coloring. He is not flamboyant, but has an erect bearing and a neat appearance. He has the look of a well-dressed bird with his muted fawn and greenish gold coloring. His ensemble is held together with the black on the tips of his wings, black and gold on his tail, and his distinguished black mask. On the outer wing feathers, there are small red tips which resemble drops of sealing wax, thus the name.

The waxwings tend to travel in groups of ten to fifty birds, except during the mating season. Both the male and female work to build their nest, which is rather loose, bulky, and crude, compared to other birds' nests. The female incubates the three to six eggs while the male stays nearby. They both feed the babies a diet of insects and small fruit, but the main diet of the adults is mostly fruit and berries. They have a passion for cherries and for berries from small trees and shrubs.

32 appliqué pieces

Color notes

One brown was used for the branches and one red for the cherries. I used two different greens to be able to distinguish between the overlapping leaves, three different gold fabrics for the bird, and black for his wing tips and mask. His tail is gold and black, edged in yellow.

Embroidered details

Eye: satin-stitch with two strands of black floss, outlined in gray
Claw: stem-stitch with two strands of black floss
Cherry stems: stem-stitch with two strands of green floss

Cedar Waxwing

BACKYARD BIRDS AND FLOWERS, photo p. 6
Add turn-under allowances.

Chimney Swift

himney swifts are sometimes confused with swallows, but it is not a swallow. The swift has a cigar-shaped body and a short stubby tail. It is all gray in color, darker on the back and lighter on the breast. Although this bird is about seven inches long, its wing span is about one foot. They are flying acrobats, living mostly on the wing—they eat in flight and mate in flight and can fly uninterrupted for up to an hour before returning to a perch to rest. They range from southern Canada south to Texas and Florida and west to the Rocky Mountains. They winter in South America.

Their nest is made of twigs, which they stick to walls or chimneys with sticky saliva. They will sometimes use an old nest that they repair. The female and the male incubate the four to six eggs, and both parents feed the young for the eighteen days they are in the nest. The bird's diet consists exclusively of flying insects.

9 appliqué pieces

Color notes

I used three values of gray for the bird: dark for the tail and outer wings, medium for wing pieces #6 and #7, and light for body piece #8. The beak was appliquéd in black.

Embroidered details

Eye: satin-stitch with two strands of dark gray floss, with a French knot in the center

Chimney Swift

VIEW FROM MY KITCHEN WINDOW, photo p. 3
Add turn-under allowances.

Chipping Sparrow

Sparrows form one of the largest of the bird groups. There are so many different species. We in suburbia are most familiar with the house sparrow. They are prolific, so people tire of seeing this same little brown bird. This is sad, because they can be so entertaining to watch. Most of the sparrows are similar in looks, with some exceptions in their markings on their head, throat, and back.

Sparrows build untidy nests of grass. These nests are often in or near our gardens, in our ground covers, in weedy fields, and in tall grass. They are not choosy. The female lays three to seven eggs, and both parents feed and care for the young. They have two to three broods a year. Grain and seeds are the sparrows' staple foods, but they will eat insects in the summer.

24 appliqué pieces

Color notes

The millet plants were appliquéd first. I used three different shades of golden tan fabric for the millet to distinguish between the different stalks.

Construction tip

For ease in making the bird, I pieced pieces #18 through #22 as a unit, then appliquéd the unit to the background.

Embroidered details

Eye: satin-stitch with two strands of brown, with a white French knot in the center

Leg and claw: stem-stitch with two strands of dark brown floss

Millet seeds: stem-stitch with two strands of floss that matches the stalks

Chipping Sparrow

BACKYARD BIRDS AND FLOWERS, photo p. 6
Add turn-under allowances.

Downy Woodpecker

The downy woodpecker is one of the most familiar, one of the smallest, and probably one of the most common woodpeckers in America. I don't know whether it is because of its size or because of its coloring, but it is one of my favorite birds.

They are friendly and not afraid of people, and they can be found in parks, gardens, farms, open woods, and in your own backyard. The male and female start their courtship in late winter and are faithful to each other, sometimes remaining paired for years. They build their nest in old and decaying tree trunks, but they will use nesting boxes. The female lays four to five eggs, which are incubated by both parents. After hatching, the babies are fed insects until ready to leave the nest at about three weeks of age. The downy's favorite food is insect larvae, but they will eat spiders, ants, beetles, and wild fruits. To attract these birds to your backyard, you can set out suet and peanut butter.

14 appliqué pieces

Color notes

I used brown for the tree trunk and gray fabric for piece #2. The breast is white, which may have to be lined if the background shadows through. The tail is black, and a striped black and white fabric was used for the wing.

Construction tips

To line the breast, use pattern #3 to cut a lightweight muslin piece, a bit smaller than the pattern. Stitching one-fourth inch in from the edge, baste the muslin piece on the background, then appliqué white fabric piece #3 over it. The easiest was to do the striped head is to appliqué pieces #4 through #9 as a unit. Then treat this unit as a single piece to appliqué it on the background.

Embroidered details

Eye: satin-stitch with two strands of black floss with a French knot in the center
Claw: stem-stitch with two strands of black floss

Downy Woodpecker

FEATHERED FRIENDS, photo p. 10
Add turn-under allowances.

Eastern Bluebird

Many old and mature trees surrounded our house in Illinois, and we had an abundance of birds. One day, I saw this incredible bird with an intensely blue body, a rust-colored breast, and a white belly. It reminded me of a Walt Disney drawing, it was so blue. How could this bird be real? It was certainly unforgettable.

Bluebirds are cavity nesters and will use holes in old trees, wooden posts, or even old woodpecker holes. The female lines the nest with fine grass, hair, feathers, and weeds and lays four to six eggs. The male feeds the young and teaches them to feed themselves while the female builds a new nest for a second brood. Over half the bluebird's diet is made up of insects, including worms, spiders, caterpillars, and ants. The balance is made up of local fruits and berries.

17 appliqué pieces

Color notes

The holly branch is one shade of brown, and the holly leaves are appliquéd with a multi-shade green fabric. I used rust for the breast and white for the belly. The body of the bird was done in two different fabrics of bright blue. The bill is black.

Construction tip

If the background shadows through piece #11, it may have to be lined. Baste a lightweight white muslin piece, cut a little smaller than pattern #11, in place on the background. Then appliqué white piece #11 over it.

Embroidered details

Eye: satin-stitch with two strands of black floss
Legs and claws: stem-stitch with two strands of black floss
Berries: satin-stitch with two strands of red floss

Eastern Bluebird

BACKYARD BIRDS AND FLOWERS, photo p. 6
Add turn-under allowances.

Eastern Meadowlark

eadowlarks are found in prairies, grasslands, farmlands, and meadows. This bird is not a lark but a member of the large blackbird family. It resembles the starling in the way it walks and flies, but the resemblance stops there because the meadowlark is a beautiful bird with a golden yellow breast and a mottled brown, gold, and white back. It is known for its song, which can be heard in the spring during courtship.

The female builds her nest in an open field or meadow and prefers a depression in a damp area. She builds a layer of coarse grasses and lines it with fine grass. She then covers the nest with a dome-shaped lid, woven from grass stems or willow leaves, to keep her nest well-concealed. The female incubates the three to six eggs, and the male helps in feeding the young.

Farmers welcome these birds, because they feed on insects, including beetles, cutworms, crickets, and grasshoppers. The meadowlark cannot be enticed to your feeders; however, if you have a large lot, seed scattered on the ground might attract them.

39 appliqué pieces

Color notes

I used one brown fabric for the branches and one green mottled fabric for all the leaves. Bright golden yellow was used for the breast, with his necklace, piece #36, appliquéd in black. The back, wing, and tail were cut from a brown and tan muted stripe. The beak is dark brown.

Embroidered details

Eye: satin-stitch with two strands of dark brown floss, surrounded by gold

Leg and claw: stem-stitch with two strands of brown floss

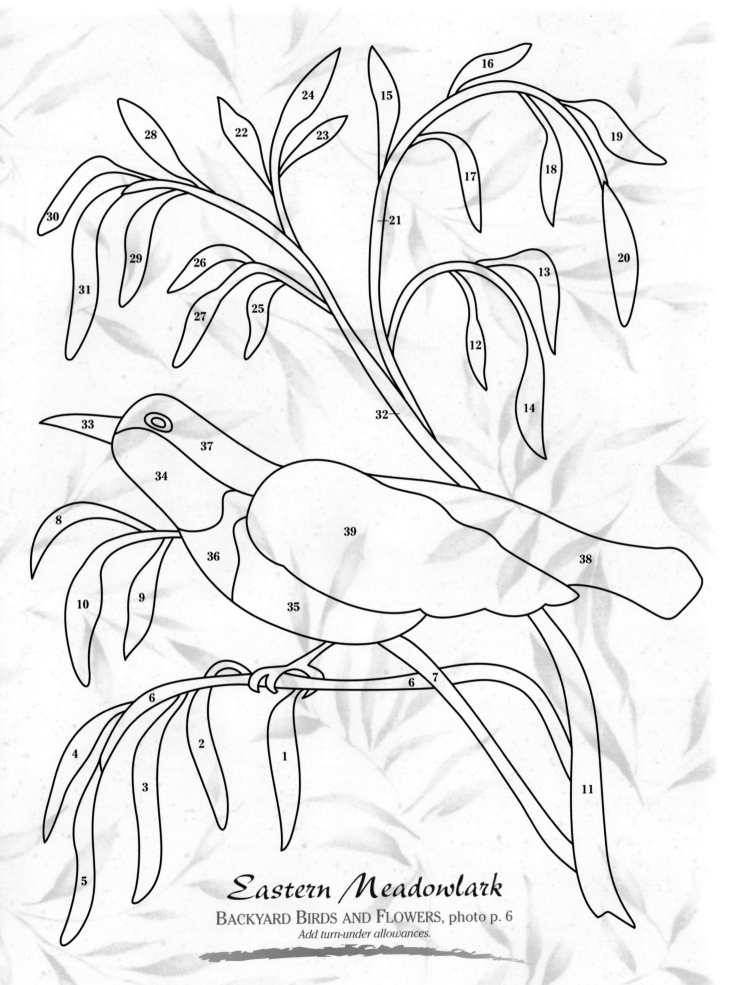

Eastern Meadowlark

BACKYARD BIRDS AND FLOWERS, photo p. 6

Add turn-under allowances.

Evening Grosbeak

The evening grosbeak resembles an over-sized goldfinch. Its feathers are more of an antique gold in color than the bright yellow of the goldfinch. It is a very showy bird with its gold and black body against a snowy landscape. They are residents of Canada, Michigan, and New England, but some of their flocks have gone as far south as the Carolinas.

The birds are very vocal during the mating season, and the female builds a nest of twigs high up in the trees. She lays three or four eggs, and while she incubates them, her mate brings all her meals to her. Both parents feed and care for the babies until they are ready to leave the nest.

The bird has a powerful beak, which is used to crunch seeds and fruit pits. Its main diet consists of seeds from trees and fruits from small trees and shrubs.

A large supply of sunflower seeds in your feeder will attract these birds to it and will keep them happy.

31 appliqué pieces

Color notes

One shade of brown was used for the branches, one shade of green for the leaves, and two shades of pink were used to distinguish between the petals. I used a dull gold for the beak and legs of the bird. The body and eyebrow are a bright yellow or gold. The head is dark brown, the tail black, and the wing black and white.

Embroidered details

Eye: satin-stitch with two strands of black floss
Stamens: stem-stitch with two strands of black floss

Evening Grosbeak

BACKYARD BIRDS AND FLOWERS, photo p. 6
Add turn-under allowances.

Allen's Hummingbird

A nectar feeder is all that is needed to attract hummingbirds to one's backyard. These little jewels come in many brilliant and metallic-looking colors. When we lived in California, we would walk in City Park in the evenings to enjoy the flowers. It was there that I saw my first hummer. I thought at first it was an insect, but they do not fly like insects. Their flight is so rapid it is hard to follow them. Hummingbirds can fly forward, zip backward, and even hover in mid-air. After mating, the female builds a tiny nest, about one inch in diameter and one inch deep. She uses spider webs to glue fine fibers and "plant down" together and to attach the nest to a tree branch. She lays two tiny eggs, which hatch in about two weeks. She feeds these tiny fly-sized babies a diet of nectar and tiny insects. The diet for hummingbirds consists mainly of nectar from flowers, some tree sap, and a few insects. To attract them to your yard, put out a plastic nectar feeder. Red is the best color; however, I have seen a bird pass by the feeder in favor of a real flower.

Allen's hummingbird is found only on the Pacific coast. It summers in Oregon and winters in southern California and Mexico.

23 appliqué pieces

Color notes

The leaves and the stem are a rich green, and the hibiscus flower and the two buds are red. The beak is black, the breast (piece #19) white or pale pink, and the back a bright green. I used gray for the wings and red for the tail and throat.

Embroidered detail

Eye: satin-stitch with two strands of black floss

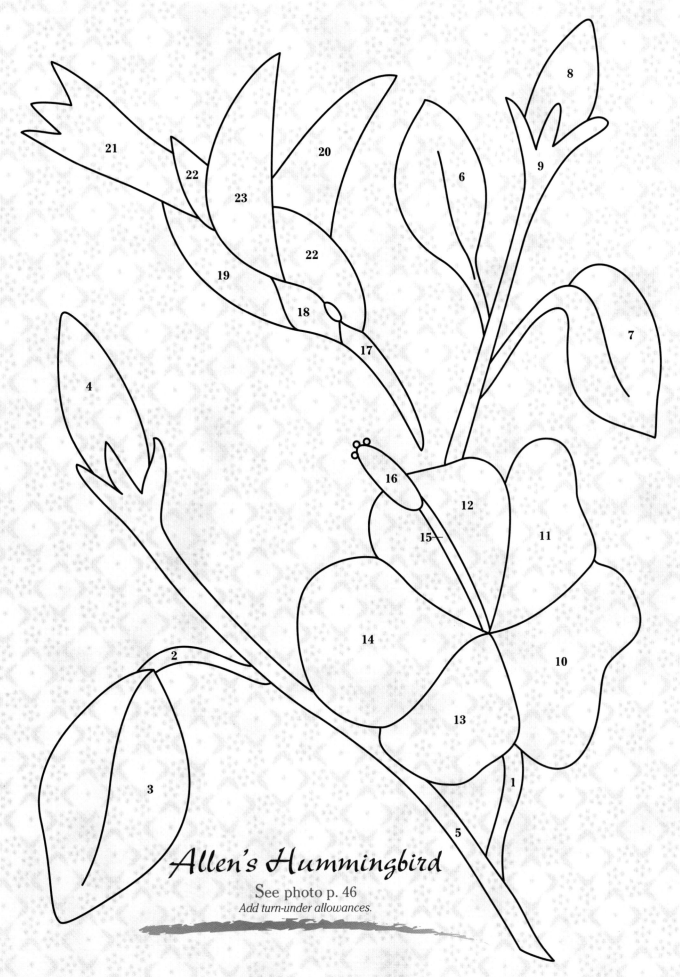

Allen's Hummingbird

See photo p. 46
Add turn-under allowances.

Ruby-Throated Hummingbird

Hummingbirds and flowers complement each other beautifully. We can create hummingbird gardens with simple backyard flowering plants. The birds are attracted to blossoms that have tubular flowers, which they pollinate while they feed on the nectar.

The ruby-throated hummingbird is the only one found east of the Mississippi River. It has the most extensive range of any of these birds, and it travels from southern Canada to Texas, Florida, and Central America for the winter.

19 appliqué pieces

Color notes

I used one green for the leaves and stem and red for the honeysuckle flowers. The bird's beak (piece #11) is black, the throat dark red, the head a bright green, and the breast (piece #13) white or pale pink. The wings and tail piece #18 are dark green, and tail pieces #16 and #17 are black.

Embroidered details

Eye: satin-stitch with two strands of black floss with a gray French knot in the center

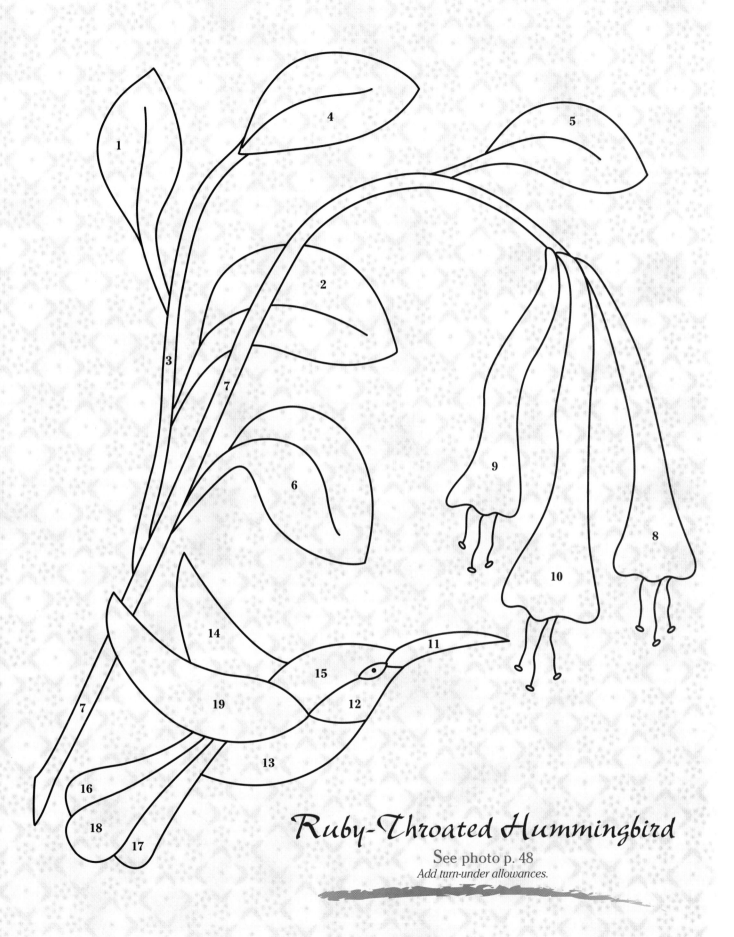

Ruby-Throated Hummingbird

See photo p. 48
Add turn-under allowances.

Indigo Bunting

The blue color of this bird is certain to attract your attention. If prizes were given for color, this bird would surely win. Compared to the male, the female is quite dull in her drab light brown. The birds range throughout the eastern United States west to Arizona. In the winter, they depart the United States, except for South Florida, for Central America but return to the north in the spring.

After mating, the female builds a well-woven nest of dried grasses, bark, and weeds and lines it with hair or feathers. The female incubates the three to five eggs herself. After the eggs hatch, both parents feed the young, which leave the nest after twelve or thirteen days. The indigo bunting has a diversified diet, which consists of about 50 percent insects, including grasshoppers, flies, and spiders, and 50 percent vegetation, including thistle seeds and small berries.

6 appliqué pieces

Color notes

Brown was used for the tree branch. For the bird, I used three shades of blue: the lightest blue for the breast and beak, medium for the head, and the darkest for the wing and the tail.

Embroidered details

Eye: satin-stitch with two strands of navy blue floss with a light gray French knot in the center
Legs: stem-stitch with two strands of dark gray

Indigo Bunting

FEATHERED FRIENDS, photo p. 10

Add turn-under allowances.

Killdeer

The killdeer is a shore bird, although it has become common in fields and pastures that are far from water. As suburbia expands into rural areas, we are finding killdeer in our gravel driveways, backyards, and rock gardens, which is where I spotted my first killdeer in its so-called nest. It will not come to a feeder, because it eats mainly grubs and insects.

The bird is about the size of a robin. Its legs are quite a bit longer than our usual backyard birds, and it has a distinctive double collar of dark brown around its neck.

The female lays three or four eggs directly on the ground, in gravel, or among rocks. The parents will vigorously guard the eggs, which are well camouflaged and difficult to find. The birds are true actors and will put on quite a show if someone gets too close. A parent bird will run from its nest, dragging a wing as if injured, to lure the intruder away.

47 appliqué pieces

Color notes

Use several shades of green for the grass to distinguish between the individual blades, and several shades of gray or tan or a combination for the rocks. Select a medium brown for the wing and a dark brown for the tail.

Construction tips

Appliqué the grass and the rocks first, then the legs and beak. Appliqué pieces #38 through #45 together as a unit before attaching them to the background. If the background fabric shadows through the white breast (#45), it may be necessary to line it with a lightweight white muslin piece, cut slightly smaller than the breast pattern. Baste the muslin piece on the background before appliquéing the pieced breast piece over it.

Embroidered details

Eye: satin-stitch with two strands of dark brown floss and a light tan French knot in the center

Killdeer

BACKYARD BIRDS AND FLOWERS, photo p. 6
Add turn-under allowances.

Mourning Dove

The name of the mourning dove comes from its sorrowful call. I consider the call more distinct than sorrowful, and because of this uniqueness, you know when one is in your yard. The dove has delicate fawn or gray coloring on its head and breast, with a deeper shade on its wings and tail. The male and female are alike in coloring. When the bird takes off in flight, its wings make a whistling sound, which is as unique as its call.

These birds mate for life, and you will seldom see a lone dove. They raise several broods each year and build their nests in many kinds of trees and vines. The nest is a bit crude, just a shallow platform of sticks and twigs. The female usually lays two eggs, and both parents share in the two-week incubation.

Adult birds feed entirely on vegetation. They are easy to attract to your backyard and to your feeders.

They will come for millet, grass seed, corn, grain, and bread crumbs. This is a gentle bird and, with its calming manner, a favorite in my yard.

17 appliqué pieces

Color notes

I used brown fabric for the log and two shades of brown for the fallen leaves. There are only five pieces in the dove, a pale fawn or beige color in the body and a darker brown color in the wings and tail. The beak is dark brown.

Embroidered details

Eye: satin-stitch with two strands of dark brown surrounded by two strands of tan in the stem stitch
Leg: stem-stitch with two strands of tan floss

Mourning Dove

BIRDERS' DELIGHT, photo p. 5
Add turn-under allowances.

Cardinal

Northern Cardinal

The cardinal is one of our most faithful backyard companions. I did not know that wild birds could be trained, or perhaps it is my husband who is trained. Every evening, as we sit in our family room to watch the news, a male cardinal comes to the glass doors and chirps at us. My husband gets up and gets the sunflower seed and feeds the bird and his mate. They are happy. This bird has a white patch on his wing about the size of a quarter, so my husband named it White-patch.

The cardinal is a perfect backyard bird because it is beautiful and has a distinctive voice. The male is scarlet red with a black mask, and the female is a light brown with tinges of red on her top notch, wings, and tail.

They love the evergreens in the yard, but our birds nest mostly in an old and very large pyracantha bush. With the thorns, I think they feel safe in its branches. Cardinals nest several times a year. The male feeds the female while she incubates the eggs, and he helps to feed the young. Sunflower seeds seem to be their favorite food, but they will eat a variety of seeds, nuts, and some insects.

22 appliqué pieces

Color notes

The bill (piece #17) is orange-red. The body of the bird is a bright red, with a deeper red in the tail and the wings. His mask is black, and the leg and claw are brown.

Construction tips

The pine cone is done first in assorted tan colors. The branches of the evergreen are appliquéd next.

Embroidered details

Eye: satin-stitch with two strands of black floss with a gray French knot in the center
Evergreen needles: stem-stitch with two strands of green floss

Northern Mockingbird

The mockingbird is the state bird of Florida. It is about ten inches long, slender, and streamlined. It is colored in two shades of gray, medium and dark. On its wings and tail there are white patches, which are most showy when the bird spreads its wings to fly. True to its name, the mockingbird is a great mimic and can imitate not only other birds, but also animals, musical instruments, and various neighborhood noises.

After mating, both the male and female take part in building a nest, usually in a shrub or small tree. They defend their brood vigorously against animals and humans who venture too close. These birds eat mainly insects, but as the summer fruits ripen, they will eat soft berries from your garden. They will sometimes visit feeders for soft foods, such as raisins.

29 appliqué pieces

Color notes

The dogwood tree is simple. I used one shade of brown for the branches, a piece of hand-dyed green for the leaves, and a mottled pink for the flowers.

There are only five pattern pieces for the bird. A light gray fabric was used for the breast, a medium gray for back, and a dark gray for the wing, tail, and beak.

Embroidered details

Eye: satin-stitch with two strands of black floss, surrounded by two strands of gold floss
Legs: stem-stitch with two strands of black floss
Dogwood centers: gold colonial or French knots

Norhtern Mockingbird

Backyard Birds and Flowers, photo p. 6
Add turn-under allowances.

Color notes

I used a variegated green for the leaves and one shade of brown for the stems. The bird was done in two shades of raspberry, light for the breast and dark for the wings and tail. The beak is light raspberry, and the leg is appliquéd with tan.

Construction tip

The white magnolia was lined to keep the background from showing through. To do this, I cut lightweight white muslin in the shape of the whole flower, but slightly smaller, and basted it in place. I then cut the petals from the flower fabric and appliquéd them over the muslin in numerical order.

Embroidered details

Eye: satin-stitch with two strands of a dark brown floss, surrounded by light beige

Stamen: stem-stitch with two strands of gold floss

P urple finches belong to the large finch family, and they are closely related and similar in appearance to the house finch. Purple finches are not really purple, but more of a raspberry color, and only the male is colorful. The female has a sparrow-like appearance with a mousy brown or gray stripe coloring.

In winter, these birds can be seen as far south as Texas and Florida, but in the spring, they head back north to New England, Upper New York, Michigan, and Canada. If you live in the middle of the country, they will stop for food on their way north or south. They nest in the north, and after mating, the female builds a cup-shaped nest of small twigs and grasses, lined with hair and soft grasses. The female lays three or four eggs, and both parents feed the young. Their diet consists wholly of vegetable matter, and they will come to your feeder if seeds are set out.

22 appliqué pieces

Purple Finch

BIRDERS' DELIGHT, photo p. 5
Add turn-under allowances.

Purple Martin

The purple martin is the largest of our swallows. It is distinctive in appearance, with its notched tail and triangular wings. The martin alternately flaps and sails, and it seems to fly in large circles. The male's back is a glossy blue black, and his breast is an iridescent purplish black. The female is duller in color, and her breast is gray.

They nest in man-made community houses and in hollow gourds. They line their nests with twigs, grasses, leaves, and feathers, and the female lays three to eight eggs. The female incubates them while the male stands guard. Both parents feed the young for about a month until they leave the nest. The purple martin has a huge appetite for flying insects, with mos-

quitoes being one of their favorites. Sometimes it is tricky to attract martins to your backyard, so if you have them, you can feel lucky.

8 appliqué pieces

Color notes

Black was used for the wings and tail and deep purple for the head and breast. The beak was appliquéd in black.

Embroidered details

Eye: satin-stitch with two strands of black floss with a light French knot in the center
Claw: stem-stitch with two strands of black floss

Purple Martin
VIEW FROM MY KITCHEN WINDOW, photo p. 3
Add turn-under allowances.

Red-Headed Woodpecker

Most people recognize this bird when they see it. It is handsome and dramatic-looking, with its all-red head, white breast, bluish black tail, and black and white wings. It has short legs and large, sharp claws, which enable the bird to cling to the bark of trees while it searches for insects. It lives in open fields near thick forests or old orchards.

Both sexes work to excavate the nest, which is chiseled in an old or dead tree, or even a utility pole. The female lays four or five eggs, and both parents take turns incubating them. They raise two broods a year. About half of the woodpecker's diet is made up of larvae, bugs, spiders, weevils, and other insects. The remainder consists of vegetable matter such as fruits, berries, and acorns. They can be attracted to your feeder with suet, peanut butter, sunflower seeds, and nuts.

16 appliqué pieces

Color notes

The body of the bird is black and white, with a crimson red head. Gray was used for the beak and claw.

Construction tip

Reverse appliqué was used for the tree: Cut the four #1 woodpecker holes from a dark brown or black fabric, about one-half inch larger than the pattern. Baste these pieces in place on the background. Mark the hole patterns on the tree-bark fabric and cut out the tree (piece #2). Place piece #2 over the holes and appliqué the outer edges of the tree in place. Carefully cut away the centers of the holes, leaving an allowance around each one. Turn the allowances under and appliqué the edges, revealing the black fabric.

Embroidered details

Eye: satin-stitch with two strands of black floss, surrounded by gray, with a gray French knot in the center

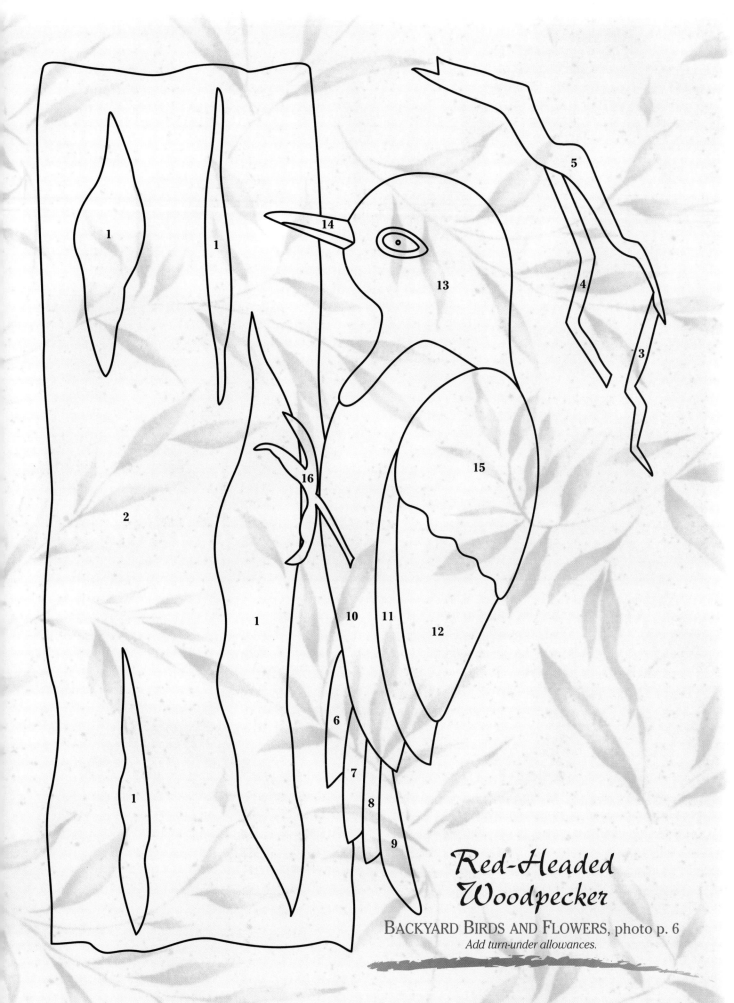

Red-Headed
Woodpecker

BACKYARD BIRDS AND FLOWERS, photo p. 6
Add turn-under allowances.

Red-Winged Blackbird

The red-winged blackbird is one of the most common birds in North America. These birds are found in every state, and their range extends from Central America into Canada. Of all the blackbirds, the redwing is one of the most attractive. The males have a jet-black body with scarlet red and gold epaulettes on their shoulders. The females are rather dull, in tan and brown with stripes on their breasts, so they look a bit like large sparrows.

Their nests are usually made in marshy areas and near or above water, although nests may be found on the ground or in bushes. They build their nests of rushes and fill in the chinks with grass and peat. Cattails are sometimes used to weave the nest together. The female lays three to five eggs, and the male stays on guard duty to protect against crows and hawks. Although it is said that they will visit feeders, I have yet to see one at ours; however, I have witnessed many birds in the grassy areas of our backyard as they feed on insects.

15 appliqué pieces

Color notes

The cattail stems and the cattails were done first. I used several shades of green for the stems to distinguish between them. The cattails are a rust color. I used two shades of black for the bird, one mottled for the body and one solid for the wing tip (piece #13). Bright gold was used for wing part #14 and a bright red for #15.

Embroidered details

Eye, beak, and claw: satin-stitch with two strands of black embroidery floss

Cattails: stem-stitch with two strands of rust floss

Red-Winged Blackbird
BACKYARD BIRDS AND FLOWERS, photo p. 6
Add turn-under allowances.

Rose-Breasted Grosbeak

The rose-breasted grosbeak is a beautiful, elegant, and distinct bird. The male is unmistakable with his black and white feathers and the triangle of rose-red on his breast. The female is brown and tan and streaked like a sparrow. The beak is large and strong and similar to the cardinal's, which assures you they are seed eating birds.

Both the male and female are accomplished singers and sing lustily during courtship. After mating, both the male and female build the nest, which is loosely constructed of twigs and lined with grasses. The female lays three to five eggs, and both sexes share the incubation and feeding of the young. The babies leave the nest when nine to twelve days old. The grosbeak's diet consists of insects, fruits, seeds, and grain.

8 appliqué pieces

Color notes

Brown was used for the tree branch and black for the head, wing, and outer portion of the tail. I used white for the breast and tail piece #6. The beak is gray and the triangle bib is rose-red.

Construction tip

The white pieces may have to be lined if the background shadows through. To line, cut pieces #1 and #6 from lightweight white muslin, a bit smaller than the pattern. Baste the muslin pieces on the background, one-fourth inch in from the edge, then appliqué white fabric pieces #1 and #6 over the muslin lining.

Embroidered details

Eye: satin-stitch with two strands of black floss, outlined with gray.
Claws: stem-stitch with two strands of gray floss

Rose-Breasted Grosbeak

FEATHERED FRIENDS, photo p. 10

Add turn-under allowances.

Scarlet Tanager

The male scarlet tanager is considered by many to be the most dramatic and the prettiest of all our backyard visitors. The male is brilliant red in color with black wings and tail, which distinguishes it from other red birds. The female is yellow-green with gray or black wings and tail. Young birds resemble their mother in color, and the males may take up to two years to attain their radiant red feathers. The birds stay hidden from view among the tall branches of mature trees, including oaks, beech, hemlocks, and the beautiful mountain ash.

The nest is built far out on a tree limb, often 40 to 50 feet high. The female lays three to four eggs. Both parents are responsible for feeding the young. Scarlet tanagers eat wild berries and other small fruits, but their main diet is made up of insects, including caterpillars. Farmers with orchards welcome these birds because they can control outbreaks of small caterpillars and gypsy moths.

37 appliqué pieces

Color notes

One green fabric was used for the leaves and one brown fabric for the branches. The mountain ash berries are scarlet red, and they are cut in one solid piece, not as individual berries. The bird's beak and the leg are appliquéd with a medium brown, while the eye is reverse appliquéd in black. The tail and wings are black, and the body is red.

Scarlet Tanager

BACKYARD BIRDS AND FLOWERS, photo p. 6
Add turn-under allowances.

Scissor-Tailed Flycatcher

Among the flycatchers the scissor-tailed is the most exotic. It has a beautiful slender body with a remarkably long and elegant tail. The coloring is pale gray on the head and salmon pink on the breast, and its wings and tail are black and white.

The birds range from the Midwest south to Texas, and they winter in Mexico, Central America, and south Florida. Their cup-shaped nest is made of twigs, weeds, grass, and twine, lined with softer materials. The female lays one egg a day for four to six days. The babies have short tails and resemble the western king-bird. Although they do eat some seeds and small fruit, the largest part of the flycatcher's diet, as the name suggests, is insects.

8 appliqué pieces

Color notes

I used pale gray for the head and salmon for the breast. A mottled black, white, and salmon fabric was used for the wings and tail. The beak and claw were appliquéd in black.

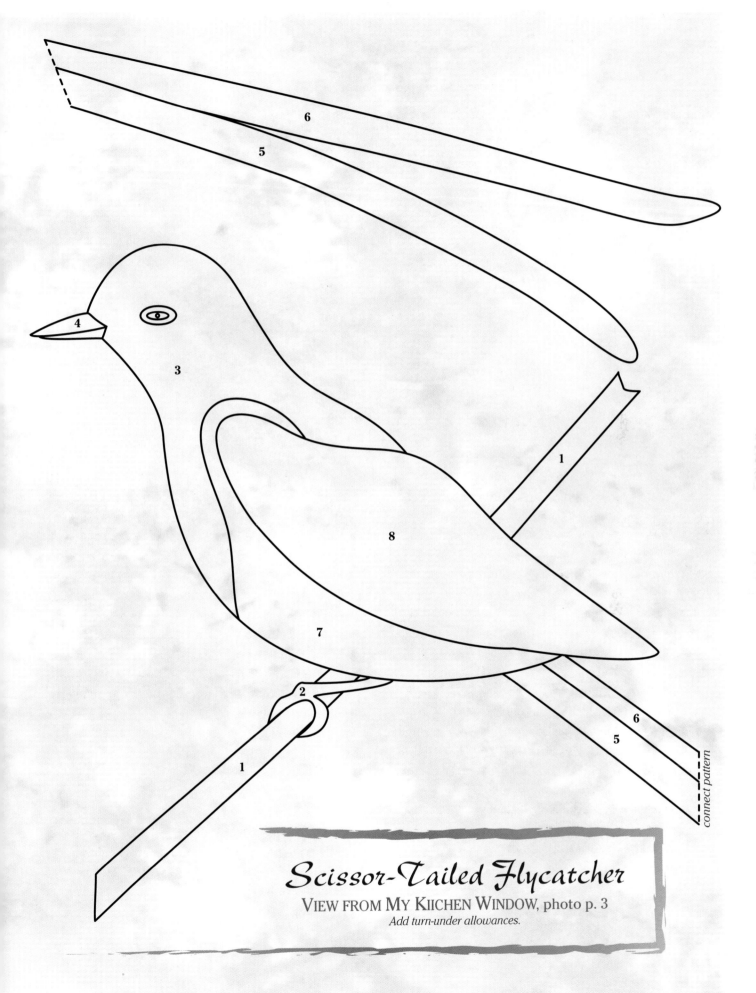

6

5

4

3

1

8

7

2

1

6

5

connect pattern

Scissor-Tailed Flycatcher

VIEW FROM MY KITCHEN WINDOW, photo p. 3

Add turn-under allowances.

Tree Swallow

ree swallows are beautiful birds. Their heads and backs are a shiny blue-green, and their breasts are pure white. Their bodies are streamlined, which helps them fly through the air rapidly in pursuit of insects, flies, and their favorite food, mosquitoes. These birds winter in the south, but return to the north in the spring.

Courtship takes place in the air. These birds do not excavate their own nesting sites, but use old nesting holes created by woodpeckers. They also nest in purple martin and bluebird houses. The female lays four to six pure white eggs in a nest lined with grasses and feathers. Both parents feed the babies. These birds are welcome, not only for their beauty in flight, but also because their appetite for insects helps keep the pests under control.

8 appliqué pieces

Color notes

The tree branch is brown. I used a deep blue-green for head piece #3 and wing piece #7. I used a pure white for the breast and a dark brown for the lower wing, tail, and beak.

Construction tips

The white breast may have to be lined if the background shadows through. To line, cut pattern piece #2 from lightweight white muslin, a bit smaller than the pattern. Baste the muslin piece on the background, one-fourth inch from the edge. Then appliqué the breast fabric over it.

Embroidered details

Eye: satin-stitch with two strands of black floss with a tan French knot in the center
Claws: stem-stitch with two strands of black floss

Tree Swallow

FEATHERED FRIENDS, photo p. 10
Add turn-under allowances.

Tufted Titmouse

Whenever I see one of these little birds, I am reminded of a very nervous person. They never seem to stay still. They will not park at a feeder, as other birds do. Instead, they fly in, grab a seed, fly off to eat it, and then come back for another seed. One has to look fast to see one of these pretty little birds. They are related to the chickadee and in fact are frequent companions with chickadees. They are all gray in color, with pale gray, almost white, on their breasts, and a deeper shade on their heads. Their wings and tails are a darker gray. Titmice are usually heard before they are seen because, with their gray clothing, they blend in with the shadows of the woods. The bird has a distinguished pointed crest, which it raises up when it becomes excited.

The nests are usually built in tree cavities, but sometimes, the birds will use a birdhouse. They line their nests with moss, fur, leaves, and grass, and the female lays four to eight eggs. The female incubates the eggs, and the male feeds her while she is sitting on the nest. The titmouse's diet consists mostly of insects, like beetles and ants, but the birds will come to your feeder for sunflower seed, peanut butter, and suet.

44 appliqué pieces

Color notes

There are only six pieces in this bird pattern. The other pieces consist of the purple coneflower and its leaves. I used one mottled green fabric for the leaves and stems, one bright purple for the flower petals, and one dark purple for the flower cone. I used four shades for the bird: near white for the breast, pale gray for the head, medium gray for the wing, and the darkest gray for the tail and beak.

Embroidered details

Eye: satin-stitch in two strands of black floss, surrounded by gray

Legs and claws: stem-stitch with two strands of dark gray

Tufted Titmouse

BACKYARD BIRDS AND FLOWERS, photo p. 6
Add turn-under allowances.

White-Breasted Nuthatch

I think of an acrobat whenever I see one of these little birds. My first encounter with the nuthatch was at our home in Illinois, which was built in a heavily wooded area. The woods were a haven for these enchanting little birds. They are small, about five to six inches in length, and they sport a black cap. The nuthatch lives on tree trunks and seems more comfortable upside down than right side up.

Nuthatches usually nest in tree crevices that they line with moss, feathers, and other soft material. The female lays five to nine eggs, and both parents incubate the eggs and tend to the young. The birds' main diet consists of insects and nuts, but they can be coaxed to a feeder with sunflower seeds and suet.

22 appliqué pieces

Color notes

I used one piece of hand-dyed green fabric for all the leaves and black for the top of his head and his beak. Two shades of blue were used: a grayish blue for the body and brighter blue for the wings and tail.

Construction tip

Reverse appliqué was used for the tree, as follows: Cut piece #1 about one-half inch larger all around than the pattern. Baste the piece on the background. Mark the #1 pattern on the tree-bark fabric and cut out the tree (piece #2). Place piece #2 over piece #1 and appliqué the outer edges of the tree in place. Carefully cut away the center of piece #1, leaving an allowance all around. Turn the allowance under and appliqué the edges, revealing the #1 fabric.

If the background fabric shadows through the white mottled breast fabric, it may be necessary to line it with a lightweight white muslin piece, cut slightly smaller than the breast pattern. Baste the muslin piece on the background before appliquéing the breast piece over it.

Embroidered details

Eye: satin-stitch with two strands of black floss, outlined in gray, with a gray French knot in the center
Leg and claw: stem-stitch with two strands of gray floss

White-Breasted Nuthatch

BACKYARD BIRDS AND FLOWERS, photo p. 6

Add turn-under allowances.

Wood Thrush

Wood thrushes are common in the eastern part of the United States. They range from southern Canada to Texas and southern Florida, where they winter. Their coloring is that of fallen leaves, and they match the undergrowth of woodlands as well as parks and gardens. Its nest, which is placed in the crotch of a small tree about 10 feet above the ground, is built of grass, weeds, dead leaves, and mud from the forest floor.

Young birds are fed by both parents. The babies leave the nest when they are about two weeks old. Obtaining most of their food on the forest floor, the thrush looks for insects, beetles, ants, and animal matter. They will also eat berries and fruit.

6 appliqué pieces

Color notes

Brown was used for the tree branch and reddish brown or cinnamon color for the head, wing, and tail. For the under part, I used a spotted tan and brown fabric.

Embroidered details

Eye: satin-stitch with two strands of dark brown, surrounded by light tan
Legs: stem-stitch with two strands of reddish brown floss

Wood Thrush

FEATHERED FRIENDS, photo p. 10

Add turn-under allowances.

Yellow-Shafted Flicker

lickers are beautiful birds, and after seeing one you will always remember it. They are large and noisy, easy to see, and fun to watch as they feed at your feeders or in your trees. Their coloring is unique with their golden-tan, speckled breast and brown wings. On its neck is a red stripe, and the male has a black mustache.

Flickers, like most woodpeckers, have a strong, pointed bill for digging into tree trunks and a strong tail for support while searching a tree trunk for its food. These birds help keep trees healthy by eating harmful insects. Flickers seek some of their food from the ground, where they eat ants, beetles, berries, and fruit. During winter, they will enjoy suet and peanut butter at your feeder. Flickers nest in the cavities of dead trees, but they are willing to use nest boxes.

14 appliqué pieces

Color notes

The bird has a tan head with a red stripe on the back of it. Its beak is dark brown with a black mustache. His breast is spotted dark brown or black on tan, the wing is very dark brown, and the tail is black.

Construction tips

Appliqué the tree stump first. To make this bird look realistic, I found it easiest to appliqué the following units before stitching them to the background:

Unit 1: piece #3 to piece #2.

Unit 2: piece #4 to piece #5; sew this unit to piece #2.

Unit 3: piece #6 to #7; sew this unit to piece #2.

Embroidered details

Eye: satin-stitch with two strands of brown floss, with a light tan French knot in the center

Claw: stem-stitch with two strands of black floss

Yellow-Shafted Flicker

BACKYARD BIRDS AND FLOWERS, photo p. 6

Add turn-under allowances.

Yellow Warbler

Within the large family of warblers, the yellow warbler is one of the most familiar and widespread. They have been called the butterflies of the bird world because of their size, about five inches, and their abundant energy. Although they are called yellow warblers, their color can be an intense orange-yellow to pale yellow. These little birds can be found from the Atlantic coast to the Pacific and from Northern Canada to the Gulf of Mexico. They prefer shrubby areas and thickets near streams, swamps, and lakes.

After mating, the males defend their territory, which can be up to 150 feet in diameter. The female builds a strong cup-shaped nest in the crotch of tree branches. She lays four to five eggs and incubates them for about 11 days. Both parents feed the four to five babies. These birds eat mainly insects but can be attracted to your yard by keeping your birdbath filled.

27 appliqué pieces

Color notes

I used one shade of brown for the branches, one shade of green for the leaves, and white for the dogwood flowers. Pink or coral could be used for the flowers if desired. Black was used for the bird's beak and leg, bright yellow for the bird's body, and dark brown for the wing and tail.

Construction tip

If white is used for the flowers, it may have to be lined to keep the background from showing through. To line, cut the petals from lightweight white muslin, a bit smaller than the pattern. Baste the muslin petals on the background one-fourth inch from the edge, then appliqué the flowers over the muslin pieces.

Embroidered details

Eye: satin-stitch with two strands of black floss
Flowers: gold French knots in the centers

Yellow Warbler

BIRDERS' DELIGHT, photo p. 5
Add turn-under allowances.

Border

BACKYARD BIRDS AND FLOWERS

The pattern for the border of BACKYARD BIRDS AND FLOWERS will fit on a 9½" wide strip (finishes 9"). The vine is quite free and flowing. You can draw free-hand curves or place them more precisely, if you prefer. The pattern pieces provided include the four little hummingbirds, the four corner motifs, and the center top and bottom motifs.

Make bias strips for the undulating vine and the longer stems. Trace the leaves and flowers on paper or template material and cut out the template pieces on the drawn lines. Trace the templates on your chosen fabrics. Add turn-under allowances (³⁄₁₆" is customary) by eye to the fabric pieces as you cut them. Make as many leaves, flowers, and hummingbirds as you want and place them at random on your vine.

1

3

2

4

6

5

Rufous

Border **Hummingbirds**

BACKYARD BIRDS AND FLOWERS
photo, pages 6 and 86
Add turn-under allowances.

2

1

4

6

7

5

3

Anna

1

4

3

7

2

6

5

Allen

1

3

4

6

5

2

Black-Chinned

Beaks and eyes are embroidered,

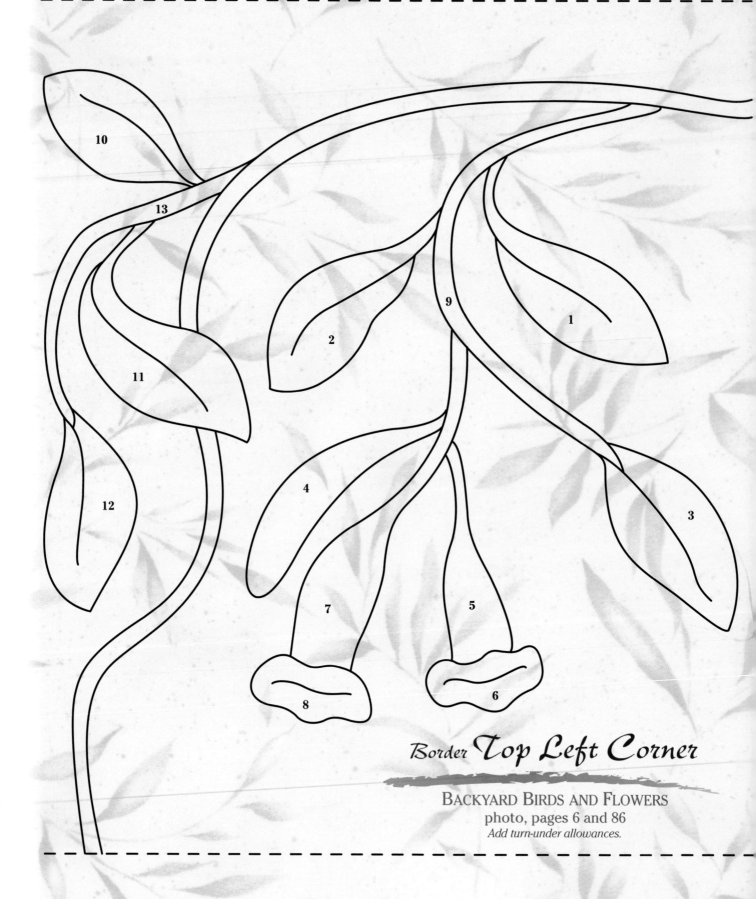

Border *Top Left Corner*

BACKYARD BIRDS AND FLOWERS
photo, pages 6 and 86
Add turn-under allowances.

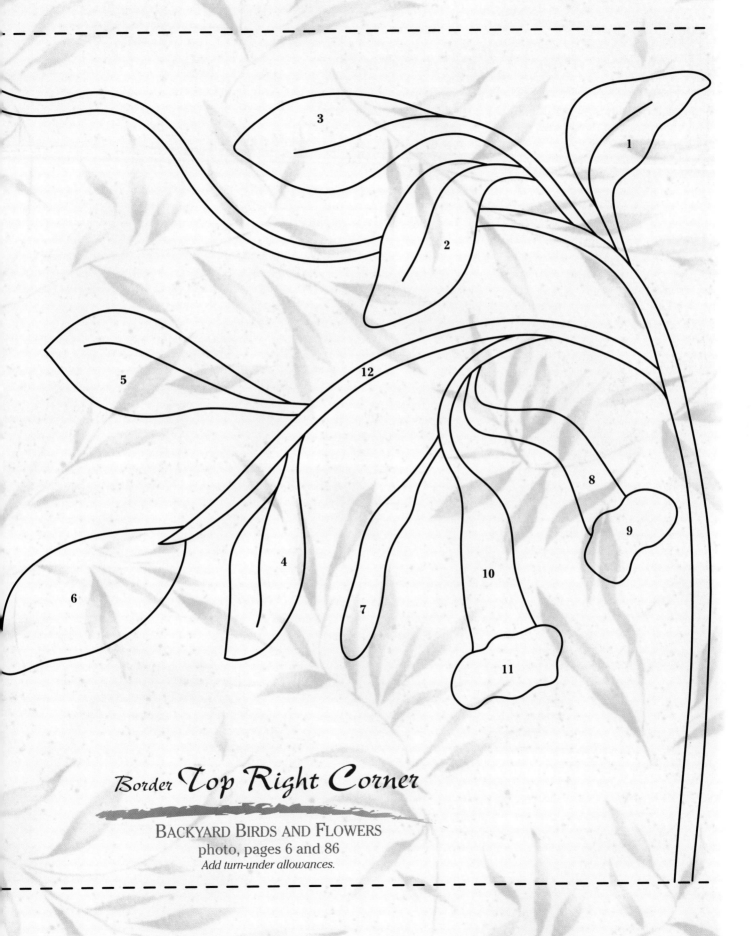

Border *Top Right Corner*

BACKYARD BIRDS AND FLOWERS
photo, pages 6 and 86
Add turn-under allowances.

Border *Bottom Left Corner*

BACKYARD BIRDS AND FLOWERS
photo, pages 6 and 86
Add turn-under allowances.

6

1

2

3

7

8

4

5

9

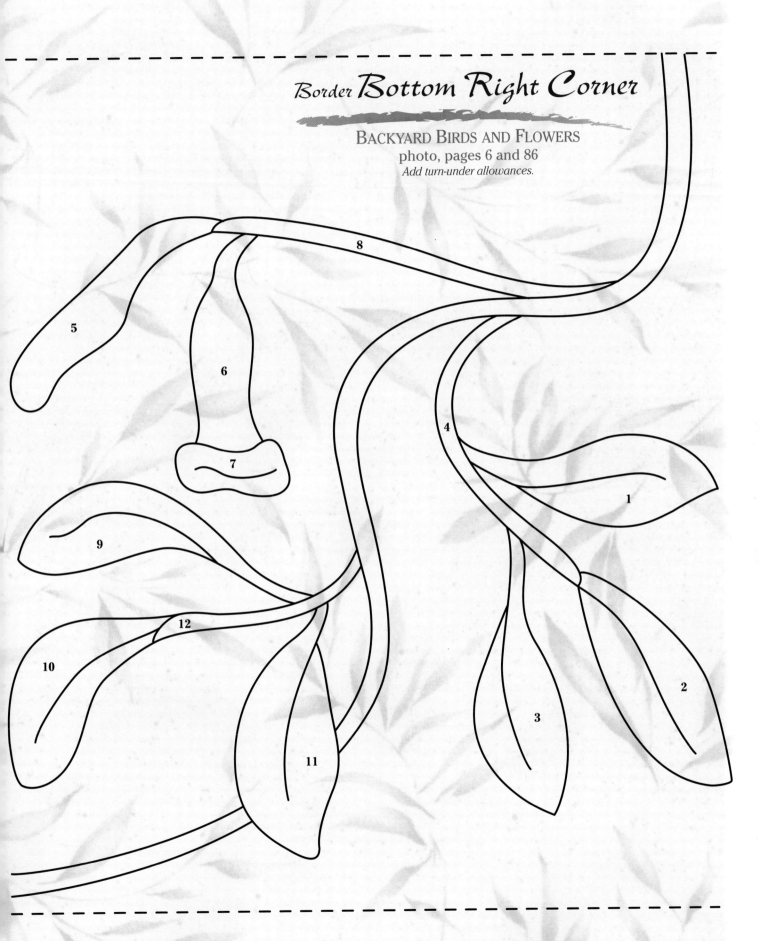

Border *Bottom Right Corner*

BACKYARD BIRDS AND FLOWERS
photo, pages 6 and 86
Add turn-under allowances.

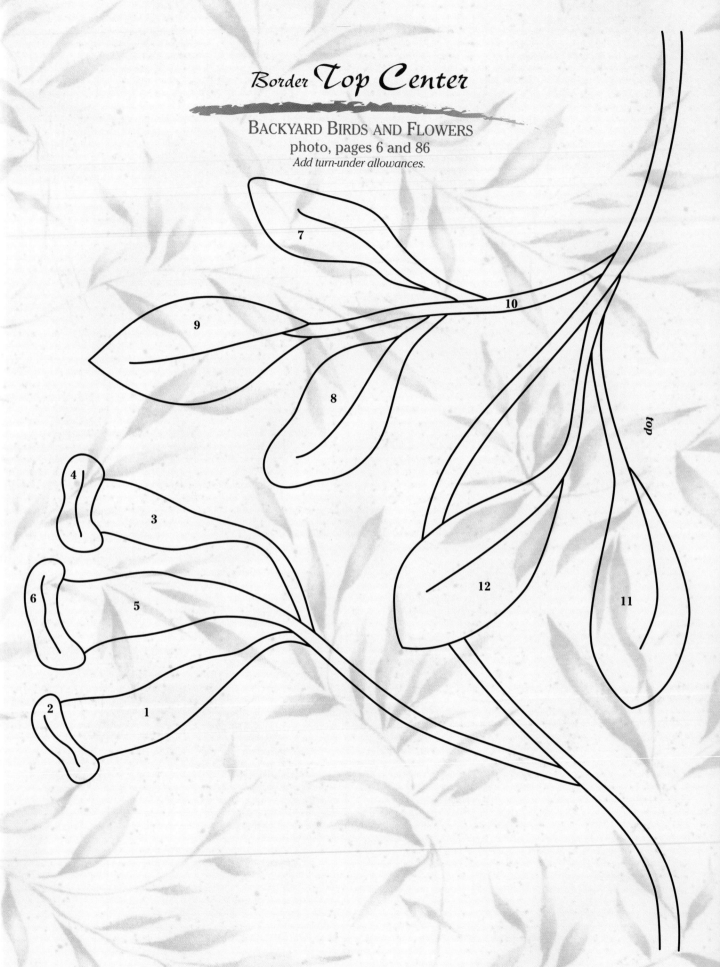

Border *Top Center*

BACKYARD BIRDS AND FLOWERS
photo, pages 6 and 86
Add turn-under allowances.

Border *Bottom Center*

BACKYARD BIRDS AND FLOWERS
photo, pages 6 and 86
Add turn-under allowances.

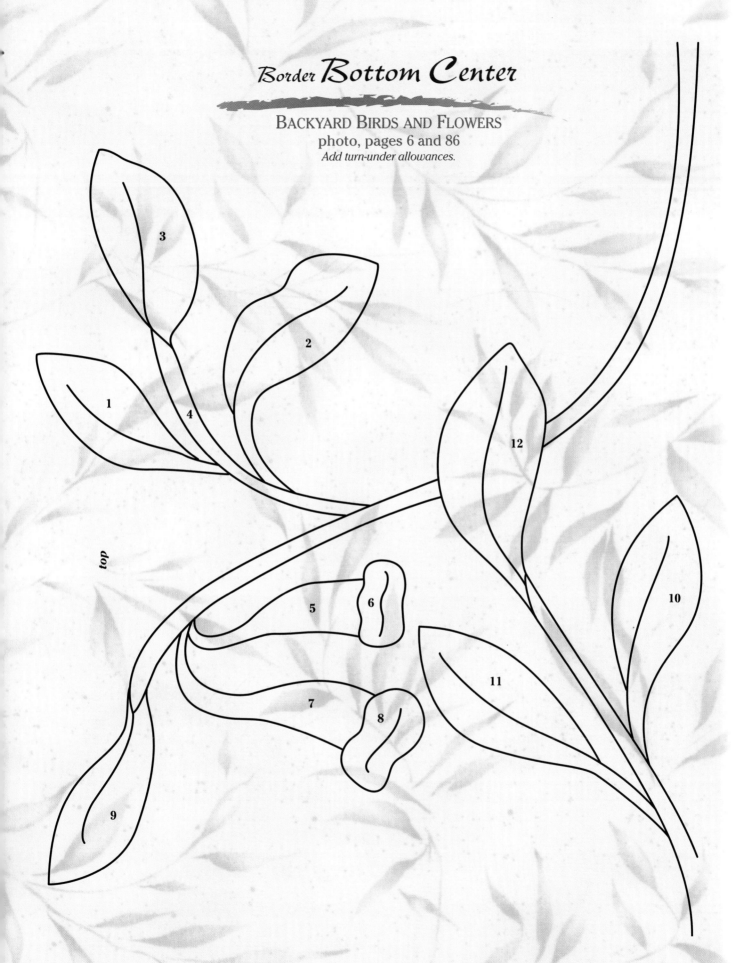

Bibliography

Adams, George. *Birdscaping Your Garden.* Emmaus, Pa.: Rodale Press, Inc., 1994.

Burton, Robert. *The Audubon Backyard Birdwatcher.* San Diego, Calif.: Thunder Bay Press, 1999.

Burton, Robert. *North American Birdfeeder Handbook,* Rev. ed. New York: Dorling Kindersley Publishing, Inc., 1995.

Ham, John. *Kitchen Table Bird Book.* Holt, Mich.: Thunder Bay Press, 1995.

Kress, Stephen W. *National Audubon Society Birder's Handbook.* New York: Dorling Kindersley Publishing, Inc., 2000.

Mahnken, Jan. *The Backyard Bird-Lovers Guide.* North Adams, Mass.: Storey Communications, Inc., 1996.

Proctor, Noble S. *Garden Birds.* Emmaus, Pa.: Rodale Press, Inc., 1985

Robbins, Chandler S., Bertel Bruun, Herbert S. Zim. *A Guide to Field Identification: Birds of North America.* New York: Golden Press, 1996.

Roth, Sally. *Attracting Birds to Your Backyard.* Emmaus, Pa.: Rodale Press, Inc., 1998.

Stokes, Donald, and Lillian Stokes. *Stokes Birdfeeder Book.* Boston: Little, Brown & Company, Ltd., 1987.

Wetmore, Alexander. *Song and Garden Birds of North America.* Washington, D.C.: National Geographic Society, 1964.

About the Author

Bea made her first quilt in 1979, for her youngest daughter, Elise, who was in college. It was in the mid-1980s that the author discovered quilting to be a wonderful art form. She found that her art studies of watercolor and oil paintings were invaluable for working with fabrics. Her fascination with nature and gardening have led to appliqué quilts of garden flowers, wildflowers, coral reefs, vegetables, fruits, birds, and more.

One of her first appliqué quilts was her CHILDREN'S CLASSIC LITERATURE QUILT, completed in 1990. It contained appliquéd illustrations of thirty-three classic children's books. This quilt has been displayed in more than fifty school libraries and in the Johnson County Central Resource Library in Kansas, near Kansas City, Missouri. Bea's daughter, Elise, sent a photo of the quilt to Barbara Bush, unbeknownst to Bea. Mrs. Bush's agenda was to fight illiteracy. First Lady Barbara Bush sent a letter that praised the quilt's contribution to children's literacy.

Bea is a member of several quilt guilds, and she teaches quilting and lectures throughout the Midwest.

Other AQS Books

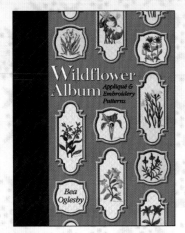

#5757   us$19.95

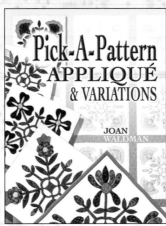

#6077   us$24.95

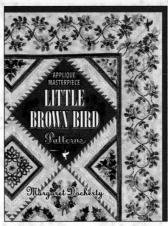

#5338   us$21.95

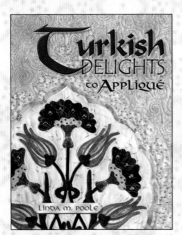

#6004   us$22.95

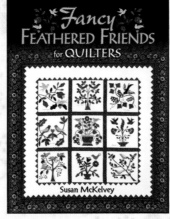

#6205   us$24.95

#5855   us$22.95

#6001   us$21.95

#5588   us$24.95

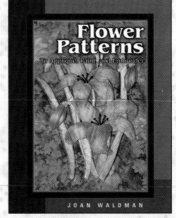

#5238   us$19.95